KB276137

# Mysterious Monsters

Happy House

# About Wise & Wide

- A systematic 6-level English reading program based on Lexile® measures
- Diverse and interesting topics chosen from the elementary curriculums of Korea and English speaking western countries
- Well-written books in various forms including fiction stories, descriptive texts, and classics retold
- The informative but original fiction stories grab your interest, leading to the easy and clear understanding of the educational content.
- Improve thinking skills with solid after-reading activities at all levels of the series.

**Wise & Wide** is a 6-level English reading program that consists of 60 books and each level is systematically divided by Lexile® measures. The Lexile® Framework for Reading is the most popular reading measuring system in American formal education curriculums and many English programs. Over 20 out of 50 states in the U.S. mark Lexile® measures directly on students' final report cards and over 300 well-known publishers adopt and use Lexile® measures.

Experience many kinds of readings written by professional writers from the U.S. and England. They used interesting topics that were carefully chosen after analyzing elementary curriculums from around the world including Korea, the U.S., England, and Australia among many others. Comprehensive after-reading activities including graphic organizers, speaking tasks, and After-reading Tests are ready for you.

### Levels in the series and their corresponding Lexile® measures

| Level | Lexile® measures | U.S. Grade |
| --- | --- | --- |
| Level 1 | Below 200L | Pre K - K |
| Level 2 | 190L - 400L | Lower Grade 1 |
| Level 3 | 350L - 530L | Upper Grade 1 |
| Level 4 | 420L - 650L | Grade 2 |
| Level 5 | 520L - 940L | Grade 3 - 4 |
| Level 6 | 830L - 1070L | Grade 5 - 6 |

* Smart Readers: Wise & Wide level 1 is applicable to the preschool level in the U.S.

* The source of the relationship between Lexile® measures and U.S. school grades: CCSS(Common Core State Standards) FOR ENGLISH LANGUAGE ARTS, APPENDIX A (2012, which is used by 45 states in the U.S.)

# Topic List

| | Level 1 | Level 2 | Level 3 | Level 4 | Level 5 | Level 6 |
|---|---|---|---|---|---|---|
| **Book 1** | Science>Biology: The hibernation of animals Story | Science>Biology: Living and nonliving things Story | Science>Biology> Animals & the Environment: Sea otters Story | Environment> Living with nature: The diver & the persimmon tree Story | Science>Biology> Animal: Amazing animals of the Amazon Story | Science>Biology: Germs, transmitted diseases Story |
| **Book 2** | Literature> World classics: Aesop's fables Story | Literature> Traditional fairy tale: Old tales about stones Story | Social Studies> Economy: To run a business to make and save money Story | Science>Biology> Plants: Photosynthesis Story | Science>Earth science: Earth's layers, earthquakes, volcanoes, and earth's atmosphere Report | Mathematics> Sequence: The golden ratio & the Fibonacci sequence Story |
| **Book 3** | Science>Physics: How shadows are formed Story | Literature> World classics: Peter Pan Story | Science>Scientific technology: Nanobots Story | Literature>Myths: World's creation stories Story | Literature> Legend: The story of King Arthur Story | Literature>Myths: Constellation myths Story |
| **Book 4** | Literature> Traditional literature: The Talmud Story | Science>Biology> Animal: Polar bears Story | Science>Biology> Animal: Mountain gorillas Story | Social Studies> Cultural anthropology: Amazing ancient cultures of the world Story | Science> Earth science: Clouds and weather Story | Literature> Human & animals: The friendship between a girl and a horse Story |
| **Book 5** | Social Studies> Ethics: Rules in daily life Story | Science>Biology: The five senses Report | Social Studies> Cultural anthropology: Astonishing festivals Report | Art>Music: Stories from two operas Story | Social Studies> World culture & history: The Renaissance Story | Sports> Board sports: Surfing & snowboarding Story |
| **Book 6** | Social Studies> World geography & travel: Tourist attractions around the world Story | Science>Biology> Animal: Dinosaurs Story | Science> Astronomy: The solar system Story | Social Studies> People: Three great people who overcame hardships Story | Science>Scientific technology: The wonderful world of robots Report | Art>Music: Composers of the Romantic Era Report |
| **Book 7** | Science> Space science: The life of astronauts Report | Social Studies> Cultural anthropology: Mythological monsters from around the world Report | Mathematics> Elementary mathematics: Numbers, measurement, shapes and data Report | Science & Social Studies> Technology & culture: Inventions from around the world Report | Art>Works of art: Famous paintings Report | Social Studies> Human & animals: Animals in action for human Report |
| **Book 8** | Social Studies> Cultural anthropology: Various living cultures of the world Story | Art>Music: Instruments in the orchestra Story | | Social Studies> History: The California Gold Rush Report | Social Studies & Science> Psychology: Psychology in everyday life Story | Literature> World classics: The Merchant of Venice Story |
| **Book 9** | | | | | | |
| **Book 10** | | | | | | |

* 10 books in each level will be published.

# How to Use This Book

## •Before Reading

You can easily find the topic and what kind of story you are about to read.

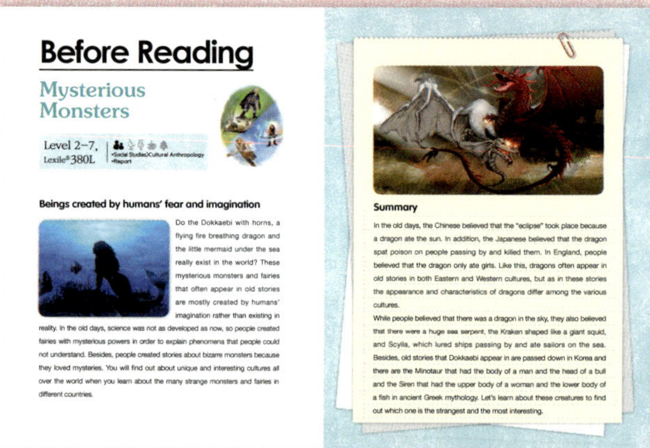

## •The text

All the stories were written by professional writers from the U.S. and England, so you will read authentic and appropriate English sentences and expressions in every book in the series.

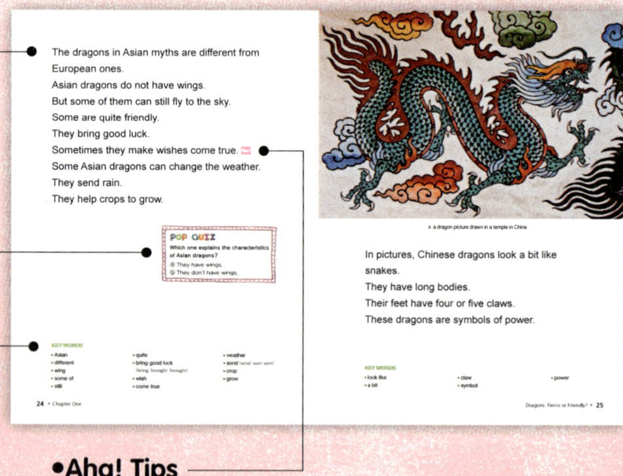

## •Pop Quiz

Check out right away if you understand what you have just read by solving a pop quiz that checks your comprehension.

## •Key Words

The key words and expressions on each page are listed for you to easily study them.

## •Aha! Tips

Download free Korean explanations at *www.ihappyhouse.co.kr* for all of the sentences marked with "Aha!". These explain cultural, scientific, and economic knowledge or they deal with aspects of English such as grammatical structures or idiomatic expressions. There are lots of "Aha! Tips" to help you understand the text.

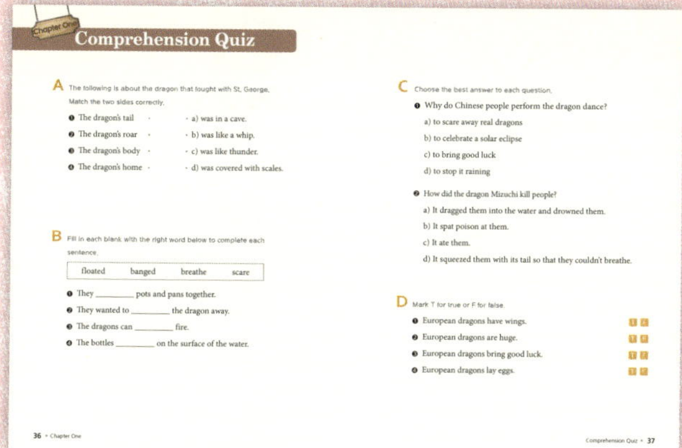

### •Comprehension Quiz

After reading one chapter, solve various questions to find out if you fully understand the content.

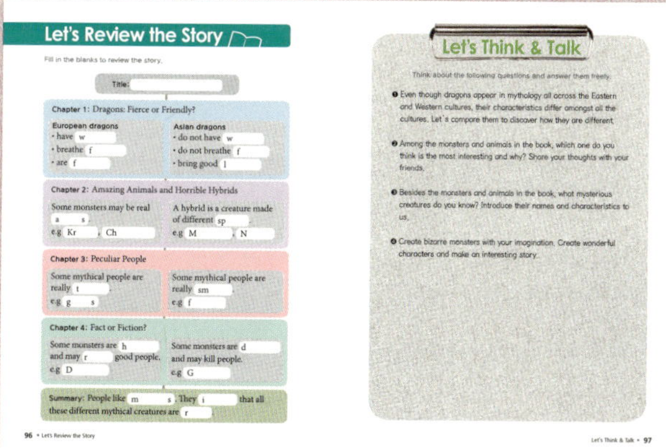

### •Let's Review the Story /
### •Let's Think & Talk

Fill in the blanks in the organizer to summarize the whole story. Express your own thinking and feelings about the story by answering the questions. You can build up logic and reasoning skills for your essay examinations in the future.

## Appendix

### Audio CD

In the CD audio book form, the texts are read vividly by American professional voice actors. (MP3 files downloaded for free)

### After-reading Test

Solve an additionally provided After-reading Test for each book.

### The Korean translation, Answer Keys, a Word Quiz, a Word List, and Aha! Tips for each book

You can download them for free at *www.ihappyhouse.co.kr* or *www.darakwon.co.kr*

# Before Reading

## Mysterious Monsters

Level 2–7,
Lexile® 380L

•Social Studies〉Cultural Anthropology
•Report

## Beings created by humans' fear and imagination

Do the Dokkaebi with horns, a flying fire breathing dragon and the little mermaid under the sea really exist in the world? These mysterious monsters and fairies that often appear in old stories are mostly created by humans' imagination rather than existing in reality. In the old days, science was not as developed as now, so people created fairies with mysterious powers in order to explain phenomena that people could not understand. Besides, people created stories about bizarre monsters because they loved mysteries. You will find out about unique and interesting cultures all over the world when you learn about the many strange monsters and fairies in different countries.

## Summary

In the old days, the Chinese believed that the "eclipse" took place because a dragon ate the sun. In addition, the Japanese believed that the dragon spat poison on people passing by and killed them. In England, people believed that the dragon only ate girls. Like this, dragons often appear in old stories in both Eastern and Western cultures, but as in these stories the appearance and characteristics of dragons differ among the various cultures.

While people believed that there was a dragon in the sky, they also believed that there were a huge sea serpent, the Kraken shaped like a giant squid, and Scylla, which lured ships passing by and ate sailors on the sea. Besides, old stories that Dokkaebi appear in are passed down in Korea and there are the Minotaur that had the body of a man and the head of a bull and the Siren that had the upper body of a woman and the lower body of a fish in ancient Greek mythology. Let's learn about these creatures to find out which one is the strangest and the most interesting.

# Mysterious Monsters

# Mysterious Monsters

# Dragons: Fierce or Friendly?

A myth is a type of story.

Many people believe it, but it is not true.

Ancient people made up myths.

They did not understand science the way we do today.

They wanted to explain why things happen.

**KEY WORDS**

- dragon
- fierce
- friendly
- myth
- a type of
- believe
- true
- ancient
- make up (make-made-made)
- understand
- science
- way
- explain
- thing
- happen
- for example
- solar eclipse
- go dark (go-went-gone)
- in the past

▲ eclipse

For example, when there is a solar eclipse, it goes dark.

The moon goes between Earth and the sun.

We know why it happens.

But in the past, people did not know.

## KEY WORDS

- Chinese
- bang
- pot
- pan
- loud

- noise
- scare ~ away
- culture
- a long time ago
- strange

- creature
- perhaps
- the best known

  (know-knew-known)

Ancient Chinese people made up a myth.

They said that a dragon was eating the sun. **Aha!**

They banged pots and pans together.

They made loud noises.

They wanted to scare the dragon away.

All cultures have myths.

They were made up a long time ago.

Many myths have strange creatures in them.

Perhaps the best known are dragons.

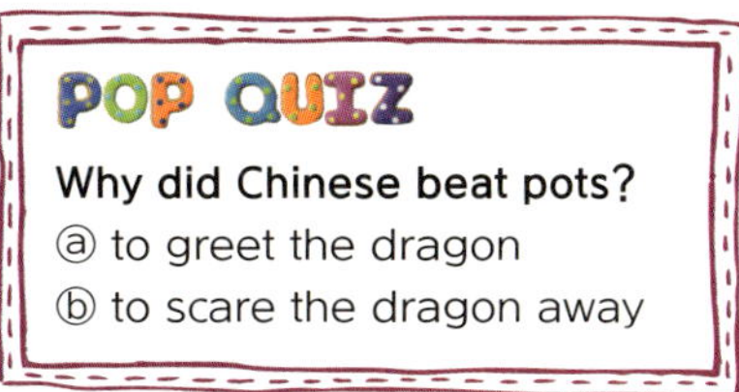

You can see dragons in movies.

You can read about them in books.

*How to Train Your Dragon* is a popular movie for children.

There is a whole series of books, too.

The author is Cressida Cowell.

They are about a boy who flies on dragons.

▲ a poster for the *How to Train Your Dragon* movie, produced in *2010*

▲ the book cover of *How to Train Your Dragon*, written by Cressida Cowell, published by Little Brown & Company



**KEY WORDS**

- train
- popular
- whole
- series
- author
- fly
- another
- well-known
- called
- inside
- lots of
- treasure

*The Hobbit* is another well-known book by J.R.R Tolkien.

In it, there is a dragon called Smaug.

Smaug lives inside a mountain with lots of treasure.

*The Hobbit* has been made into three movies.

In European myths, dragons are flying lizards.

They are huge.

They can breathe fire.

They lay eggs.

Sometimes they have magical powers.

They frighten people and
kill them.

The flag of Wales shows
a red dragon.

It comes from a myth.

▲ flag of Wales

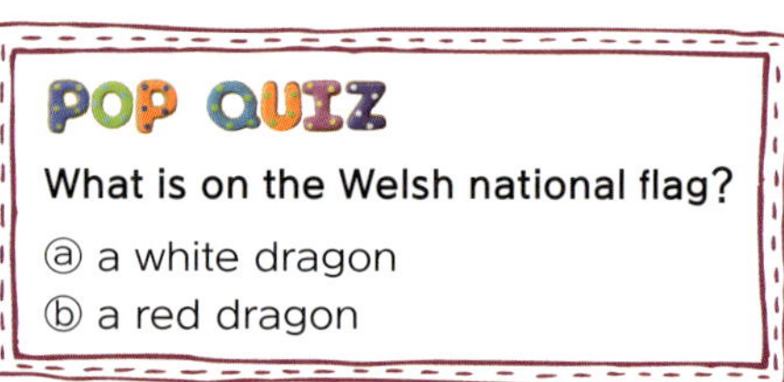

POP QUIZ

**What is on the Welsh national flag?**

ⓐ a white dragon

ⓑ a red dragon

**KEY WORDS**

- European
- lizard
- huge
- breathe fire
- **lay eggs** (lay-laid-laid)
- sometimes
- magical
- power

- frighten
- kill
- flag
- Wales
- show
- **come from** (come-came-come)
- England

In the myth, there are two dragons.

One is red, and one is white.

The red dragon of Wales kills the white dragon of England. **Aha!**

the United Kingdom ▶

In England, there is a famous myth.

It tells of St. George and a dragon.

St. George was a brave knight.

He lived hundreds of years ago.

He traveled around on his horse.

He came to the country of Libya.

A dragon lived there.

Everyone was afraid of the dragon.

Each day, the dragon ate a young girl.



**KEY WORDS**

- famous
- St.
- brave
- knight

- hundreds of
- travel around
- country
- Libya

- be afraid of
- each
- **eat** (eat-ate-eaten)

Now, all the girls had gone.

Only the princess was left.

"Is there anyone who can kill the dragon?" said
the king.

St. George wanted to save the princess.

He went to the cave where the dragon lived.

The dragon rushed out.

Its tail was like a huge whip.

Its roar was like thunder.

**POP QUIZ**

**Why was the princess the only girl left in Libya?**

ⓐ All the other girls had been eaten by the dragon.
ⓑ All the other girls had run away.

**KEY WORDS**

- go
- princess
- **leave** (leave-left-left)
- save

- cave
- rush out
- tail
- like

- whip
- roar
- thunder

St. George was very brave.

He tried to stab the dragon with his spear.

But the dragon's body was covered with scales.

They were so hard that the spear broke.

**KEY WORDS**

- **try to**
- **stab** (stab-stabbed-stabbed)
- **spear**
- **be covered with**
- **scale**
- **hard**
- **break** (break-broke-broken)

St. George fell off his horse.

He stabbed the dragon with his sword.

The dragon spat poison onto him.

St. George's armor split in two!

Then, St. George saw something.

There were no scales under the dragon's front leg.

St. George got up.

He ran toward the dragon.

He stabbed the dragon with his sword under its
front leg.

The dragon fell down dead.

St. George was a hero!

## KEY WORDS

- **fall off** (fall-fell-fallen)
- **sword**
- **spit** (spit-spat-spat)
- **poison**

- **armor**
- **split** (split-split-split)
- **get up** (get-got-gotten)
- **toward**

- **fall down dead**
- **hero**

The dragons in Asian myths are different from European ones.

Asian dragons do not have wings.

But some of them can still fly to the sky.

Some are quite friendly.

They bring good luck.

Sometimes they make wishes come true. 

Some Asian dragons can change the weather.

They send rain.

They help crops to grow.



**KEY WORDS**

- Asian
- different
- wing
- some of
- still

- quite
- bring good luck
  (bring-brought-brought)
- wish
- come true

- weather
- send (send-sent-sent)
- crop
- grow

▲ a dragon picture drawn in a temple in China

In pictures, Chinese dragons look a bit like snakes.

They have long bodies.

Their feet have four or five claws.

These dragons are symbols of power.



- look like
- a bit
- claw
- symbol
- power

Even today, at Chinese New Year, a dragon
dance is performed.
A team of dancers stands beneath a long dragon
costume.
They hold it up on poles.
They move the poles about.
It looks as though the dragon is alive.
It seems to move about.

Chinese people still believe that this dance brings them good luck.

The longer the dragon, the more good luck they will have.

A long time ago, the dragon dance was performed to bring rain.

People thought that the dance made it rain on their fields.

It made their crops grow.



**KEY WORDS**

- even
- new year
- perform
- a team of
- dancer
- beneath
- costume
- **hold ~ up** (hold-held-held)

- pole
- move ~ about
- as though
- alive
- seem
- **think** (think-thought-thought)
- field

There are dragon myths in Japan, too.

There is a myth about a Japanese water dragon.

Its name was Mizuchi.

It lived in a river.

When people passed, it spat poison at them.

The people died.

One day, a man came to the river.

His name was Agatamori.

He threw three bottles made from

gourds into the river.

They floated on the surface of

the water.

"Dragon!" he called out.

"Can you sink these bottles?

If you can, I will leave you alone.

If you cannot, I will kill you."

▲ gourd

## POP QUIZ

What did the Japanese dragon do to people passing by?

ⓐ It spat poison at them.
ⓑ It took them to the river.

**KEY WORDS**

- Japan
- Japanese
- pass
- one day
- man
- **throw** (throw-threw-thrown)
- bottle

- made from
- gourd
- float
- surface
- call out
- **sink** (sink-sank-sunk)
- leave ~ alone

The dragon changed into a deer.

It tried to sink the bottles.

But they kept floating back to the surface. Aha!

So Agatamori killed the dragon.

All the other water dragons
lived in a cave.

The cave was at the bottom
of the river.

Agatamori killed them all, too.

The river water turned into
blood.

▲ Agatamori described in *Zenken kojitsu*: *kōshō* published in Japan in 1903 (By Kikuchi, Yōsai (November 28, 1781 - June 16, 1878) and Yamashita, Shigetami [Public domain or Public domain], via Wikimedia Commons)

## POP QUIZ

**Where did all other water dragons live?**

ⓐ in a cave at the bottom of the river
ⓑ in a cave at the bottom of the sea

### KEY WORDS

- change into
- deer
- keep + *Verb*-ing (keep-kept-kept)
- back to

- other
- at the bottom of
- turn into
- blood

In the U.S.A., there is a myth about the Piasa Bird.

The story was first told by a Native American Indian tribe. Aha!

They hunted in a valley.

They fished in a river.

They were safe and happy.

But then a strange creature arrived.

It had wings and its body was covered with scales.

It had horns and red eyes.

Its tail was so long that it passed around its body.

Then, its tail went over its head and between its legs.

The people became afraid.

Does the Piasa sound like a dragon?

▲ Piasa Bird

**KEY WORDS**

- **U.S.A.** (United States of America)
- first
- Native American
- Indian tribe
- hunt
- valley
- fish
- safe
- arrive
- horn
- around
- over
- between
- sound like

There are hundreds of dragon myths.

They come from all around the world.

This makes people today wonder if dragons were once real. `Aha!`

Perhaps they were a type of dinosaur.

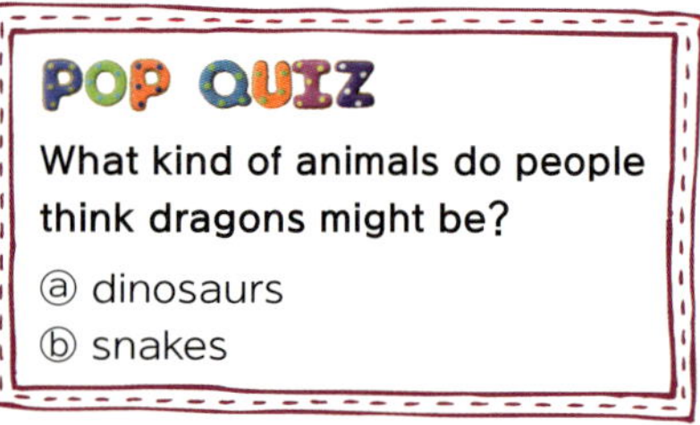



**KEY WORDS**

- all around the world
- wonder if
- once
- real
- dinosaur

# Comprehension Quiz

**A** The following is about the dragon that fought with St. George. Match the two sides correctly.

❶ The dragon's tail  •          • a) was in a cave.

❷ The dragon's roar  •          • b) was like a whip.

❸ The dragon's body  •          • c) was like thunder.

❹ The dragon's home  •          • d) was covered with scales.

**B** Fill in each blank with the right word below to complete each sentence.

| floated | banged | breathe | scare |
| --- | --- | --- | --- |

❶ They ___________ pots and pans together.

❷ They wanted to ___________ the dragon away.

❸ The dragons can ___________ fire.

❹ The bottles ___________ on the surface of the water.

 Choose the best answer to each question.

**❶** Why do Chinese people perform the dragon dance?

a) to scare away real dragons

b) to celebrate a solar eclipse

c) to bring good luck

d) to stop it raining

**❷** How did the dragon Mizuchi kill people?

a) It dragged them into the water and drowned them.

b) It spat poison at them.

c) It ate them.

d) It squeezed them with its tail so that they couldn't breathe.


**D** Mark T for true or F for false.

**❶** European dragons have wings.      T F

**❷** European dragons are huge.      T F

**❸** European dragons bring good luck.      T F

**❹** European dragons lay eggs.      T F

# Amazing Animals and Horrible Hybrids

Most of the creatures in myths are not real.

But some of them might be!

Ancient maps had pictures of sea monsters on them.

There are ancient stories of sailors who said that they had seen a huge sea serpent.

▲ oarfish

Modern scientists think that the sea serpent was a giant oarfish.

This fish can grow to 11m long.

It looks like a sea serpent.

But it is a real animal.



**KEY WORDS**

- amazing
- horrible
- hybrid
- most of
- monster
- sailor
- sea serpent
- modern
- scientist
- giant
- oarfish

▲ a picture drawn by imagining the Kraken attacking a ship

The Kraken is another mythical sea creature.

People said that it attacked boats.

They said that its body was as big as an island. Aha!

Some sailors said that they had seen it.

They said that it was a mile long.

Modern scientists think that the Kraken was a giant squid.

The giant squid can grow to 18m long.

It is a real animal.

The Kappa is from
a Japanese myth.
Pictures of the Kappa
show a strange
creature.
It has a beak.
It has the body of a
tortoise.
Its legs are like frogs' legs.

▲ a picture that described Kappa
(By 竜斎閑人正澄 (Japanese) (scanned from ISBN 978-4-336-
05055-7.) [Public domain], via Wikimedia Commons)

## POP QUIZ

**What do scientists think the Kraken was?**

ⓐ a squid
ⓑ a salamander

**KEY WORDS**

- Kraken
- mythical
- attack

- as big as
- island
- mile

- giant squid
- beak
- tortoise

It has a hollow on the top of its head.

The hollow is filled with water.

If the water dries up, the Kappa loses its powers.

People used to think that the Kappa ate children.

Modern scientists think that the Kappa was a

giant salamander.

The giant salamander

can grow to 5m long.

It is a real animal.

▲ salamander



- hollow
- on the top of
- be filled with
- dry up (dry-dried-dried)
- lose one's power (lose-lost-lost)
- used to
- salamander
- not always
- Chupacabra
- goatsucker
- This is because ~
- suck
- dead
- hole

Myths are not always ancient.

A modern myth tells of the Chupacabra.

It lives in North and South America.

Sometimes it is called the "goatsucker."

This is because it sucks the blood from goats.

The goats are left dead.

They have two small holes in their necks.

The Chupacabra was first seen in 1995.

Some people say that it looks like a lizard.

It has sharp spines on its back.

Others say that it looks like a dog with no fur.

Some scientists think that it is a coyote.

They think that it has a skin disease.

This makes it look strange.

Perhaps it is a real animal, too.

▲ a picture that described Chupacabra
(By LeCire (Image:Chupacabras.JPG)
[Public domain], via Wikimedia)

▲ coyote

Some mythical creatures are definitely not real!

Many have body parts from different animals.

Others have some animal and some human body

parts.

A creature that is made of different species is

called a hybrid. Aha!

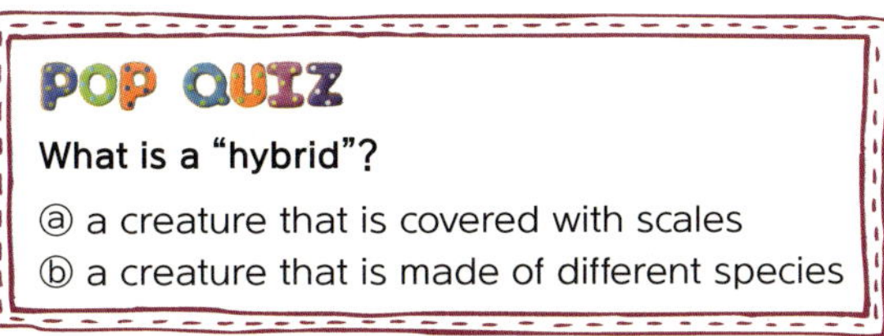


**KEY WORDS**

- be seen
- sharp
- spine
- back
- fur

- coyote
- skin
- disease
- definitely
- body part

- human
- be made of
- species

Ancient Greek myths contain lots of hybrids.

The Minotaur has a man's body and a bull's head.

It lives in a labyrinth under the ground.

It eats people.

▲ Minotaur

▲ Hercules and Minotaur



**KEY WORDS**

- Greek
- contain
- lots of
- Minotaur
- bull
- labyrinth
- under the ground
- centaur

A centaur has a horse's body and a man's head.

In some pictures, centaurs have only two legs.

In other pictures, centaurs have four legs.

▲ centaur

There are hybrids in myths from other cultures, too.

Mermaids have a woman's body.

But instead of legs, they have the tail of a fish.

They appear in myths all over the world.

There is even a modern movie called *The Little Mermaid*.

▲ mermaid

In ancient Greek myths, mermaids are called
Sirens.

They sing a beautiful song.

Sailors hear it.

They go closer to listen.

They fall in love with the beautiful Sirens.

The Sirens pull them underwater.

The sailors drown.

Many hybrids are made from different animals.

A Chinese myth tells of the Nian.

It lived a long time ago.

The Nian had the body of a bull.

It had the head of a lion.

It lived in the mountains.

The Nian was very fierce.

At the end of the winter, the Nian was hungry.

It came down from the mountains.

It went to the villages.

It ate children.

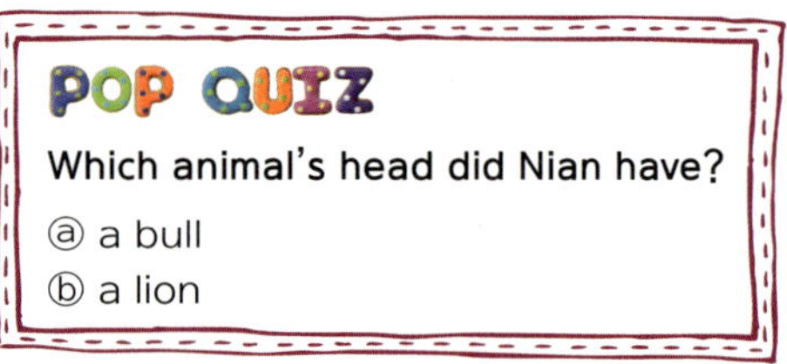

The people were afraid.

They left food outside their houses.

They hoped that the Nian would take the food.

They hoped that it would not eat their children.

Then, the people discovered something.

The Nian was afraid of three things.

It was afraid of fire, loud noises, and the color red.

So each spring, the people lit red lanterns.

They let off firecrackers.

They put red decorations in their windows.

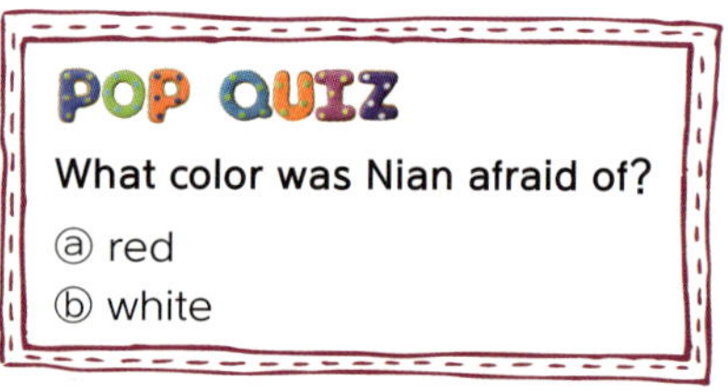

After that, the Nian never came to the village
again.
Ever since, Chinese New Year is celebrated this
way.
There are fireworks and red decorations.

The Grootslang is from a South African myth.

The word means "great snake."

In the myth, the Grootslang was once very powerful.

The gods did not like this.

They decided to take away its power.

So they split the Grootslang into two animals.

It became the elephant and the snake.

But one Grootslang escaped.

Some people say that it is still alive.

It lives in a cave full of diamonds.

Nobody has ever found this cave.

Some people say that nobody has found it

because it does not exist.

Others say that the cave is real.

But the Grootslang guards it well.

**KEY WORDS**

- African
- word
- mean
- powerful
- god

- decide
- take away
- escape
- full of
- diamond

- nobody
- find (find-found-found)
- exist
- guard

# Comprehension Quiz

**A** Mark T for true or F for false.

❶ The Nian was afraid of fire.　　　　　T　F

❷ The Nian was afraid of water.　　　　T　F

❸ The Nian was afraid of the color blue.　　T　F

❹ The Nian was afraid of loud noises.　　T　F

**B** Circle the right word for each underlined part.

❶ Modern scientists think that the Kraken was a giant (<u>oarfish</u> / <u>squid</u>).

❷ The Minotaur has a (<u>man's</u> / <u>woman's</u>) body and a (<u>lion's</u> / <u>bull's</u>) head.

❸ A centaur has a (<u>bull's</u> / <u>horse's</u>) body and a (<u>man's</u> / <u>woman's</u>) head.

❹ Mermaids have a (<u>man's</u> / <u>woman's</u>) body and the tail of a (<u>fish</u> / <u>lizard</u>).

 Choose the best answer to each question.

**❶** Which of these does the Kappa NOT have?

a) a beak

b) the legs of a frog

c) the body of a tortoise

d) some wings

**❷** In the myth about the Nian, why did the Chinese people leave food outside their houses?

a) They wanted their children to eat the food.

b) They wanted the Nian to eat the food instead of their children.

c) They wanted to keep the food cool.

d) They wanted the Nian to come closer to their homes.

**D** Fill in each blank with the right word below to complete each sentence.

| beautiful | island | sharp | modern |
|---|---|---|---|

**❶** Sirens sing a ____________ song.

**❷** A ____________ myth tells of the Chupacabra.

**❸** The Chupacabra has ____________ spines on its back.

**❹** The Kraken's body was as big as an ____________.

# Peculiar People

Strange types of people are found in myths.

Often, they are very small.

Sometimes, they are very big.

Giants are found in myths all over the world.

They look like humans.

But they are very tall.

Giants have great strength.

They can throw rocks.

They pull up trees by the roots.

Some of them can hold up the sky.

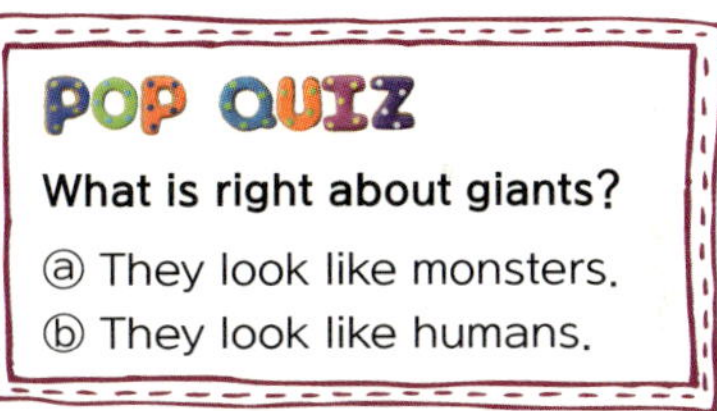


**KEY WORDS**

- peculiar
- often
- strength

- throw
- rock
- pull up

- by the roots

Cyclopes appear in Greek and Roman myths.

They are giants.

Each has one eye in the middle of his forehead.

The Greek hero Odysseus tricked one of them.

It wanted to kill him.

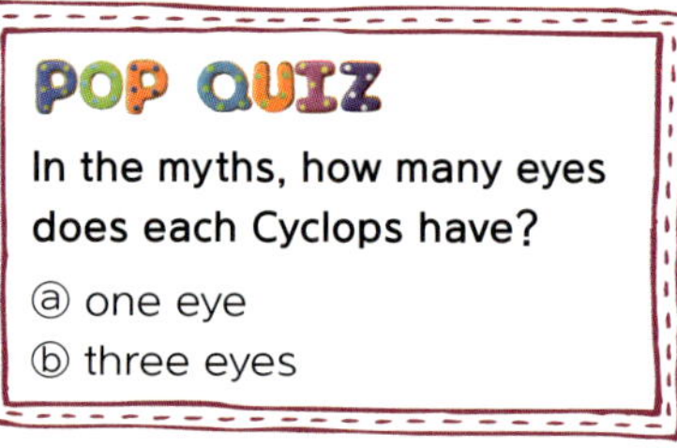


**KEY WORDS**

- Cyclopes
- Roman
- in the middle of
- forehead

- Odysseus
- trick
- blind
- so that

- burning
- branch

But he blinded the Cyclops so that it couldn't
see. 

He put a burning branch into the Cyclops' eye.
Odysseus escaped.

There are lots of giants in Norse myths.

They live in a land of giants.

It is called Jotunheim.

The myths say that most giants are ugly.

But some of them are beautiful.

They all fight with gods and humans.

They get angry easily.

They like to destroy things.

Fairies are perhaps the most well-known mythical people.

In modern movies and books, fairies have wings.

They glow with light.

They are often kind.

Fairy godmothers make wishes come true.

Tooth fairies take away children's teeth when they have come out. **Aha!**

The fairies leave money instead.

But in ancient European myths, fairies are
frightening.

They have magical powers.

Sometimes they take a human baby from its
cradle.

They put in one of their own babies instead.

It is called a "changeling."

**KEY WORDS**

- frightening
- cradle
- changeling

Fairies come in all shapes and sizes.

Some are tiny.

Others are human-sized.

Many are beautiful.

But some are ugly.

It is impossible to say what a fairy looks like!

In Ireland, people say that the fairies were once gods.

They ruled the country.

They had four magic objects.

The first was a magic stone. 

If a true king of Ireland stepped on it, it would scream.

The second was a magic sword.

Anyone struck with it would die.



**KEY WORDS**

- Ireland
- rule
- object
- magic
- step on
- scream
- second
- **strike** (strike-struck-struck)

The third was
a magic sling shot.

When a stone
was fired from it,
it always hit the
target.

The fourth was
a magic cauldron.
It always had
food in it.
The food never
ran out.

But one day, other people invaded Ireland.

The gods were allowed to stay.

But they had to live underground.

They became small, and hid away.

They were rarely seen.

There are still people living in Ireland who say

that they have seen the "little people."



**KEY WORDS**

- third
- sling shot
- be fired from
- **hit the target** (hit-hit-hit)
- fourth
- cauldron
- **run out** (run-ran-run)

- invade
- be allowed to
- stay
- underground
- **hide away** (hide-hid-hidden)
- rarely

There are stories of "little people" all over the world.

In Hawaii, there are the Menehune.

In the myths, they lived there before anyone else.

They were good at building things.

Each of the Menehune was good at one special thing.

One was good at carving stone.

Another was good at making things from wood.

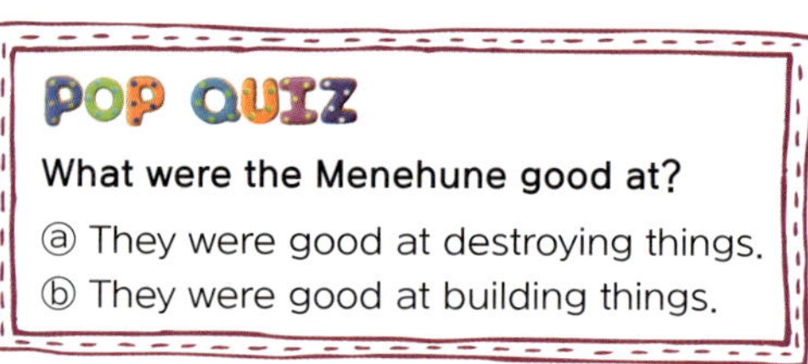



**KEY WORDS**

- Hawaii
- anyone else
- be good at
- build
- special

- carve
- wood
- wonderful
- fish pond
- dam

- road
- temple
- at nightfall
- finish
- sunrise

Together, they made wonderful things.

They made fish ponds and dams.

They made roads and temples.

They began to build at nightfall.

If it wasn't finished by sunrise, they stopped
working and never finished it.

The Zulus of Africa tell of even smaller people.

The Abatwa are so tiny that they ride on ants.

Only a few people can see them.

Very young children can see them.

Pregnant women and magicians can see them, too.




- Zulu
- ride on (ride-rode-ridden)
- only a few
- pregnant
- women
- magician
- Norway
- troll
- behind
- bridge
- traditional tales
- such as
- gruff
- unhelpful
- clever
- shine (shine-shone-shone)

In Norway, there are myths about trolls.

They live in caves or behind rocks.

Sometimes they live under bridges.

They appear in traditional tales such as *The Three Billy Goats Gruff*.

They are often unhelpful to humans.

Trolls are often old and ugly.

They are not very clever.

But they have a lot of gold.

It is hidden away in caves.

They come out at night.

If the sun shines on them, they turn into stone.

J.R.R. Tolkien has written about trolls in *The Hobbit*.

They turn into stone when the sun shines on them.

There are some rocks in Norway that are a strange shape.

People say that they were once trolls.

But now they have been turned into stone forever.

There is a famous rock called "Troll's Tongue."

▲ Troll's Tongue

Trolls appear in some books and movies, too.
In the movie *Frozen*, there are trolls that are
friendly and helpful.

A mountain troll appears in the book and movie,
*Harry Potter and the Philosopher's Stone*.
It is ugly and unfriendly, and definitely not helpful!

Some myths tell of humans.

But they are not ordinary humans.

The Abarimon are said to have backward feet.

Everything else about them is normal.

Only their feet are different.

Despite this, they can run very fast. 

They live in the Himalayas.

They are used to the pure air there.

They cannot breathe anywhere else.

So only people who go to the Himalayas can see them.

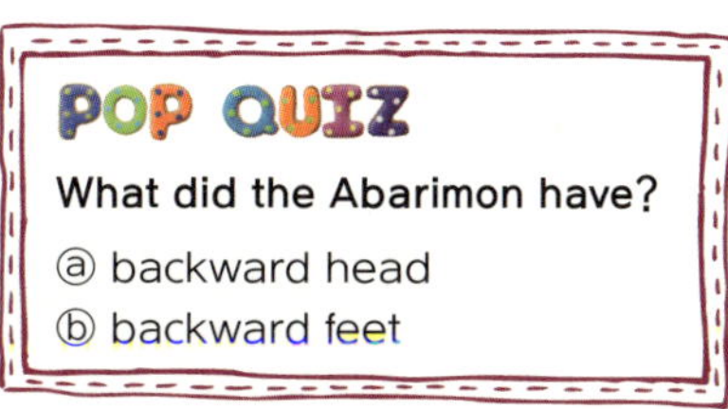


**KEY WORDS**

- ordinary
- backward
- everything else
- normal
- despite

- the Himalayas
- be used to
- pure
- anywhere else

# Chapter Three

# Comprehension Quiz

**A** The following is about things that Irish fairies had. Match the two sides correctly.

❶ The magic stone     •

❷ The magic sword     •

❸ The magic sling shot  •

❹ The magic cauldron  •

• a) always hit the target when a stone was fired from it.

• b) would scream if a true king of Ireland stepped on it.

• c) always had food in it.

• d) would kill anyone who was struck with it.

**B** Choose the best answer to each question.

❶ When did the Menehune do their work?

a) in the morning          b) in the afternoon

c) at night              d) at any time

❷ What happens to trolls when the sun shines on them?

a) They melt away.        b) They turn into humans.

c) They catch fire.         d) They turn into stone.

C  Solve the crossword puzzle.



❶ In Ireland, the fairies had four magic o________.

❸ The giants like to d________ things.

❺ Other people i________ Ireland.



❷ There is a famous rock called "Troll's T________."

❹ The Greek hero Odysseus t________ one of Cyclopes.

# Fact or Fiction?

Some mythical creatures are not like animals.

They are not like humans.

They are different from anything else.

Korean myths tell of the Dokkaebi.

Nobody knows exactly what they look like. **Aha!**

They change their appearance.

But most people agree that they are frightening.

They also agree that some Dokkaebi only have one leg.



**KEY WORDS**

- fact
- fiction
- anything else
- Korean
- Dokkaebi

- exactly
- what ~ look like
- appearance
- agree

A Dokkaebi likes to wrestle.

But there is an easy way to defeat it.

You can push it over from the right side.

You can also hook its leg and pull.

This will make it fall over.

Dokkaebi have magical things.

They have magical hats.

The hats make them invisible.

They have magical clubs.

The clubs can get anything the Dokkaebi want.

**KEY WORDS**

- wrestle
- defeat
- push ~ over
- right side
- hook

- pull
- fall over
- invisible
- club
- steal (steal-stole-stolen)

- harmless
- reward
- play a joke
- play a trick

Dokkaebi use the club to steal things from other people.

They steal things by using magic.

A Dokkaebi may look frightening.

But often it is harmless.

Sometimes it rewards good people.

It likes to play jokes and tricks.

Another famous monster is in a poem.

The poem is called *Beowulf*.

It is an ancient English poem.

It was written hundreds of years ago. 

Beowulf is the name of a brave man.

In the poem, he lived in Scandinavia.

A terrible monster lived there, too.

The monster was called Grendel.

Grendel means "The Destroyer."

The poem says that Grendel was "very terrible to look upon."

Nobody knows exactly what he looked like.

But he was very fierce.

The Danish king Hrothgar held feasts in a great hall.

Afterwards, he and his men slept there.

Each time, Grendel came and killed most of them.

Hrothgar survived.

Brave Beowulf went to fight Grendel.

They had a long battle.

Beowulf killed Grendel.

He cut off Grendel's head to show that the monster was dead. Aha!

Hrothgar was very pleased.

He gave Beowulf lots of gifts.

In Scotland, there is a story about The Headless Trunk.

This is a monstrous creature without a head.

It was said to haunt a particular road.

It attacked male travellers and killed them.

But it never attacked women or children.

Nobody walked along that road after sunset.

But a man called Big John decided to try and fight the monster.

**KEY WORDS**

- battle
- cut off (cut-cut-cut)
- pleased
- Scotland
- headless
- trunk
- monstrous
- haunt
- particular
- male (↔ female)
- traveller
- walk along
- sunset

He walked along the road after sunset.

The monster met him, and they had a terrible
fight.

It went on all night.

Big John held onto the monster tightly.

He wanted to see what it looked like.

He waited for the sun to rise, so he could see it.

The Headless Trunk begged Big John to let it go.

It did not want the light of the sun to fall on it.

The monster promised to leave and never come back.

At last, Big John agreed to let it go.

The Headless Trunk ran away into the mist, howling.

It was never seen again.

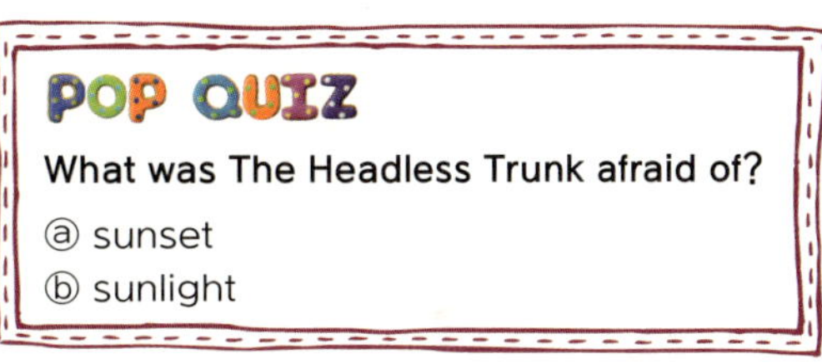


**KEY WORDS**

- go on
- all night
- hold onto
- tightly
- wait for
- rise
- beg
- let ~ go (let-let-let)
- fall on
- promise
- come back
- at last
- run away
- mist
- howl

Greek myths tell of a monster called Scylla.

She lived at the same time as the hero,

Odysseus.

This monster was female.

In the myths, she had six long necks.

At the end of each neck was a head. Aha!

Each head had three rows of sharp teeth.

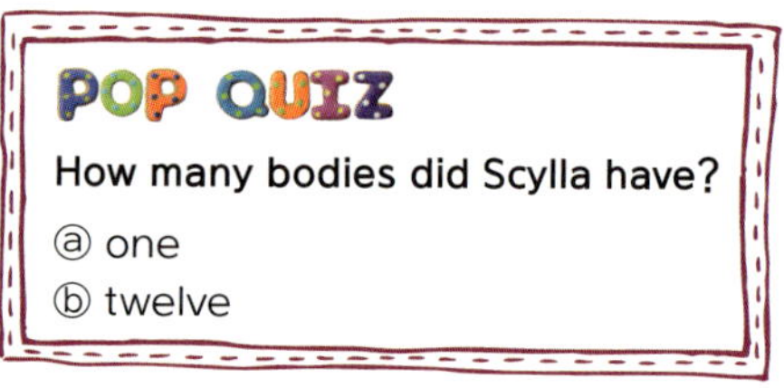

Scylla had twelve feet.

She only had one body.

Her body was made of the heads of barking dogs.

She lived on a rock.

The rock was in a cave by the sea.

Scylla could not leave the rock.

Nearby was a dangerous whirlpool.

Sailors kept away from the whirlpool. 

Their boats took them near Scylla's cave.

When they came near, Scylla crushed them against the rock.

Then, she ate the sailors.

Why are there so many myths about monsters?
Why do people like to hear about strange creatures?
Perhaps it is because people like mysteries.
They imagine that all these different mythical creatures are real.



**KEY WORDS**

- nearby
- dangerous
- whirlpool
- keep away from
- near
- crush
- against
- mystery
- imagine

# Chapter Four

# Comprehension Quiz

**A** Circle the right word for each underlined part.

❶ Scylla had one (<u>body / neck</u>).

❷ Scylla had six long (<u>legs / necks</u>).

❸ Scylla had twelve (<u>hands / feet</u>).

❹ Scylla had three rows of (<u>teeth / eyes</u>) on each head.

**B** Mark T for true or F for false.

❶ The poem *Beowulf* was written hundreds of years ago.　　T　F

❷ Beowulf was a terrible monster.　　T　F

❸ Grendel held feasts in a great hall.　　T　F

❹ Grendel killed the men who were asleep in the hall.　　T　F

**C** Choose the best answer to each question.

**❶** How can you defeat a Dokkaebi? Choose two answers.

a) Steal its magic hat.

b) Push it over from the right side.

c) Push it over from the left side.

d) Hook its leg and pull.

**❷** Where was Scylla's rock?

a) in a cave by the sea

b) in a forest by a lake

c) in a cave by a river

d) in a lake by a mountain

**D** Fill in each blank with the right word below to complete each sentence.

| attacked | crushed | held | went |
| --- | --- | --- | --- |

**❶** The Danish king Hrothgar ___________ feasts in a great hall.

**❷** Brave Beowulf ___________ to fight Grendel.

**❸** The Headless Trunk ___________ male travellers and killed them.

**❹** Scylla ___________ boats against the rock.

# Let's Review the Story

Fill in the blanks to review the story.

Title: 

**Chapter 1:** Dragons: Fierce or Friendly?

**European dragons**
- have w
- breathe f
- are f

**Asian dragons**
- do not have w
- do not breathe f
- bring good l

**Chapter 2:** Amazing Animals and Horrible Hybrids

Some monsters may be real a s .
e.g Kr , Ch

A hybrid is a creature made of different sp .
e.g M , N

**Chapter 3:** Peculiar People

Some mythical people are really t .
e.g g s

Some mythical people are really sm .
e.g f

**Chapter 4:** Fact or Fiction?

Some monsters are h and may r good people.
e.g D

Some monsters are d and may kill people.
e.g G

**Summary:** People like m s . They i that all these different mythical creatures are r .

# Let's Think & Talk

**Think about the following questions and answer them freely.**

❶ Even though dragons appear in mythology all across the Eastern and Western cultures, their characteristics differ amongst all the cultures. Let's compare them to discover how they are different.

❷ Among the monsters and animals in the book, which one do you think is the most interesting and why? Share your thoughts with your friends.

❸ Besides the monsters and animals in the book, what mysterious creatures do you know? Introduce their names and characteristics to us.

❹ Create bizarre monsters with your imagination. Create wonderful characters and make an interesting story.

# Let's Review the Story

**Title:** Mysterious Monsters

**Chapter 1:** Dragons: Fierce or Friendly?

**European dragons**
- have wings
- breathe fire
- are fierce

**Asian dragons**
- do not have wings
- do not breathe fire
- bring good luck

**Chapter 2:** Amazing Animals and Horrible Hybrids

Some monsters may be real animal s .
e.g Kraken , Chupacabra

A hybrid is a creature made of different species .
e.g Minotaur , Nian

**Chapter 3:** Peculiar People

Some mythical people are really tall .
e.g g iant s

Some mythical people are really small .
e.g fairies

**Chapter 4:** Fact or Fiction?

Some monsters are harmless and may reward good people.
e.g Dokkaebi

Some monsters are dangerous and may kill people.
e.g Grendel

**Summary:** People like mysterie s . They imagine that all these different mythical creatures are real .

# After-reading Test

- Mysterious Monsters
- Level 2
- 18 Questions

(Vocabulary 5 / Reading Comprehension 10 /

Sentence Structure & Grammar 3)

1.  Which pair has the wrong past tense form of the listed verb?
    ① break – broke
    ② throw – threw
    ③ leave – leaved
    ④ become – became

2.  What does "frightening" mean in the following sentence?

    A Dokkaebi may look frightening.

    ① scary            ② strange
    ③ friendly         ④ helpful

3.  Which of the following explains the meaning of "hybrid" best?
    ① a creature that eats people
    ② a creature that is made of different species
    ③ a creature that can breathe on land and underwater
    ④ a creature that has a skin disease

4.  Which of the following explains the meaning of "changeling" best?
    ① a type of baby bed
    ② an ugly baby
    ③ a fairy baby
    ④ a troll baby

5.  What is the common word for the two blanks?

> • The dragon rushed _______.
>
> • The food never ran _______.

① to
② out
③ into
④ for

6.  Why did ancient people make up myths?
   ① They wanted to frighten people.
   ② They wanted to explain why things happen.
   ③ They wanted to protect themselves from monsters.
   ④ They wanted to entertain each other.

7.  Why did the Native American Indians become afraid?
   ① The river flooded the land near their homes.
   ② Hunters came to the valley near their homes.
   ③ A cave appeared in the ground near their homes.
   ④ The Piasa Bird arrived near their homes.

8.  In the South African myth, who took away the Grootslang's power?
   ① gods
   ② humans
   ③ snakes
   ④ elephants

9.  In the South African myth, what is inside the Grootslang's cave?
   ① gold
   ② lanterns
   ③ diamonds
   ④ gods

10. In the Greek myth, how did Odysseus escape from the Cyclops?
   ① He blinded it.
   ② He tied it up.
   ③ He killed it.
   ④ He put it to sleep.

11. What do tooth fairies leave when they take children's teeth away?
   ① babies                    ② stones
   ③ candy                     ④ money

12. What is strange about the Abarimon?
   ① They only have one eye each.
   ② They are very small.
   ③ They breathe underwater.
   ④ They have backward feet.

13. Who cannot see the Abatwa?
   ① old men                   ② pregnant women
   ③ young children            ④ magicians

14. Why does nobody know what exactly Dokkaebi look like?
   ① Nobody has ever seen one.
   ② They can change their appearance.
   ③ They are invisible.
   ④ People who have seen one forget what they look like.

15. Which people did The Headless Trunk attack?
① men                          ② women
③ children                     ④ everyone

※ Choose the wrong part of the sentence. (16~17)

16.
But they kept to float back to the surface.
    ①      ②      ③    ④

17.
They said that its body was as big to an island.
    ①    ②                      ③      ④

18. What is the proper word for the blank?

Sometimes they ______________ wishes come true.

① come                         ② take
③ make                         ④ bring

**Sarah J. Dodd**

Sarah J. Dodd is an experienced primary school teacher who resides in the UK, but has also lived and taught in Australia. She has a PhD in Science and a certificate in Creative Writing. She has published several books for children: "An Angel Anyway" (Anyway Press, 2008) the "Little Angels" series (Lion Children's Books, 2009/10), "The Lion Picture Bible" (Lion Children's Books, 2015) and "Legs: the tale of a meerkat lost and found" (Lion Children's Books, 2015). Her poetry for children has also been highly commended and published in the anthology "Let in the Stars" (Manchester Metropolitan University, 2014).
She is currently working on further picture books for the very young, and a novel for older children.

# Mysterious Monsters

Written by Sarah J. Dodd
Illustrated by Hyeyeong Kim

First Published in April 2016

Editorial Manager: Juyon Choi
Editors: Juyon Choi, Hyunjeong Kim, Kyunghee Jang, Jiyeong Park
Designer: Eunhee Lee
Cover Designer: Eunhee Lee

Published and distributed by

Darakwon Bldg., 64-1 Jandari-ro, Mapo-gu, Seoul, Korea 04031
Tel: 82-2-736-2031(ext. 250)     Fax: 82-2-732-2037
Homepage: www.ihappyhouse.co.kr
Publisher: Kyudo Chung



ISBN: 978-89-6653-404-3 18740 / 978-89-6653-156-1 18740(set)

[Components]
• 1 Audio CD (Recording Studio: Aram)
• Answer Keys & Korean Translation: Free download at www.ihappyhouse.co.kr